Illustrated by: *Vidya Vasudevan*

Publication Date: October 2023

No part of this publication may be reproduced or transmitted in any form or by any means, electronic or mechanical, including photocopying, recording, or any information storage and retrieval system, without permission in writing from the publisher.

Copyright © 2023 by Dottie Ferri

Long Valley, NJ

All Rights Reserved

Publisher: D&L Books LLC

ISBN 978-1-7379131-8-4

SUMMARY

Christmas season is upon us, and Tim is filled with excitement! He's determined to have the best Christmas ever, and it starts with a search for a ***VERY SPECIAL*** Christmas tree. But Tim has no idea what's in store for him, and how special this Christmas ***WILL TRULY BE!***

"We are all in a book, and someone's turning the pages..."

Tim's Best Christmas Ever!

~ A Christmas "Mystery" Adventure ~

Dottie Ferri

Illustrated by: Vidya Vasudevan

As Christmas approached, the thought became clear,

That the holiday season was really *quite* near!

Happy thoughts filled my head as I thought of the day,

Filled with lots of ***great presents*** that was coming my way!

The days fill with planning for those who now wait,
For that special day coming, *but we can't hesitate!*
There are presents to buy, and the choice of a tree...
Oh my*, that* decision is met with such glee!

As we waited and waited, the day finally came,

When we looked for that tree *that wasn't the same!*

This year would be different, as we made up our minds,

To pick a tree *this* time that would be an unusual kind!

We went off to the woods as it started to snow,

'Cause it seems so much better when the land is "aglow"…

With the beautiful glistening of snowflakes piled high,

On the rows of tall pines that before were so dry.

But as we picked out our tree, I thought it was strange...

How the trunk was *so bent*... so how could we arrange??

That part of the tree so it fit in the stand,

And it could stand upright, and the tree could look *grand*?!

But we learned not to worry, as the tree took its place,

In the room, Christmas morning, where we all would then race...

Finding gifts that were left underneath twinkly lights,

As we play with our toys, and the day turns to "night".

As we looked at the tree in all of its glory,

I couldn't help thinking that it held back a story...

It seemed something strange was going on with that tree,

And when I looked hard, *I was able to see...*

There *was* a big hole in the trunk on the right...

It was *shaped like a door*, and it was such an odd sight!

When you looked oh so closely, you could really then see,

What looked like a doorway, tucked inside of the tree!

I thought I would need to check into this more,

And would wait for the time I was free to explore,

Whatever was hiding inside of this tree...

Was a mystery to solve, *and it was left up to me!*

That night I couldn't help notice, as we slept in our beds,

The noises from the tree that whirled in my head!

So I crept down the stairs, for a better view to see,

What was *really* going on inside this *mysterious tree?*

I saw a dim light shining through the tiniest of doors..

The door that I spotted on the tree the night before.

I got on my knees so I could see the doorway really clear.

I couldn't be *too noisy*...and **THAT WAS** my biggest fear!

But as I started thinking, that this must be just a dream,
And anything I was seeing couldn't be as it now seemed...
I saw a *little* guy... twinkly eyes, with toes curled up...
Sitting on the littlest chair, sipping tea from the tiniest cup!

With a silver beard, and on his head, an awesome floppy hat,
As it tumbled down far from the place, where on his head it sat.
A cuter guy you'd never see... as small as the tiniest elf...
But he *didn't* look like the "*Elf*" I knew, that sits upon my shelf!
The one that visits every year and hides all through our home...
And then we go in search of him, wherever he may roam!

I wanted to ask him questions, and to find out *would he stay?*

I hoped that he would tell me if I stayed out of his way.

So I clenched my fist, and knocked on his door, and hoped that he would greet me...

And to my surprise he did *just that* and acted glad to meet me!

My name is *"Tim"* I told him, as I managed a big smile.

"I'm so very glad to meet you! Will you be staying for a while?"

He said he would, because he had a real big job to do...

For someone very dear to him, and I could help him too!

Who could this be? *I feared to ask*.... I didn't want to pry!

"Give me a hint" I said to him, but he answered with a sigh.

"Very soon you'll learn, and I will share, the things you need to know",

"I'll share with you what I'm able to, but then you *need to go!*"

A Christmas Tree starts as a seed, put in the ground to grow.

It's put amidst the evergreens, all placed in a neat row.

I make a home within the tree, and guard it 'til it's tall,

I have a job to see this through, because I am so small!

Until the day a family takes the tree to its new home,

I guard it so I know it's safe,

'Cause I'm the "Christmas Gnome"!

I left the little guy that night, although I didn't want to....

What was this *"big job"* he talked about, known only by a few?

I kept the **"Gnome"** my secret, hoping he would soon reveal...

Who is this "dear friend" he held so close? And how should that make me feel?

So many questions left me with my mind still wanting more...

That I found myself visiting every night, as I knocked upon his door!

One night as we were talking, he told me to admire,
All the things my *Mom* and *Dad* would do, and never seem to tire!
He told me that I need to show my **"thanks"** in different ways…
For all the things they do for me, counting all the yesterdays.

I didn't sleep at all that night, as thoughts raced through my mind,
Of all the things to be grateful for, from those who are so kind.
I decided on a *special* gift, so I wrote them both a letter,
And after I got done with that, *I was feeling so much better!*

The words of thanks for all they've done were not to be ignored,

I felt so good while writing them ....and then headed for the door.

After writing them the letter, and making the words all fit...

I brought it to the *Christmas Gnome*, and hoped his light was lit!

He took the letter from me, and told me I should *"go"*.

I watched him put it in a sack, as he turned his light down low.

Christmas Eve was now upon us, and we tumbled into bed.
I wondered where my letter went, and it wouldn't leave my head!
The Gnome now had my letter, but where would it now fit?...
I crept downstairs to relieve my mind, to sit by the tree a bit.

And then there was before me, a really *awesome sight!!...*
I saw "my" *Christmas Gnome* , as I squeezed my eyes real tight!
He sat upon the shoulder of a man *all dressed in red...*
But as I watched, *I knew I should be hustling back to bed!*

He gave my letter to a jolly guy, who had the biggest grin!

As he crossed the room where the stockings lay, and stuck my letter in.

"Your job is done," I heard him say, "and it's time for you to go!"

"You helped our Tim by showing him the one thing he *must* know…."

"Christmas comes but once a year, but *always* should it be,

To appreciate the ones you love, and never fail to see…

The caring that is freely given without a thought in mind..

Of all the the gifts along the way, because they are so kind.

I had to linger just awhile, so I could trust my eyes…

And watched the *Gnome* and *"Man in Red"* exchange their warm goodbyes.

And so, on Christmas morning, I couldn't help but see,

The happiness in my parents' eyes, as they looked upon the tree.

They found my letter and smiled, finding what it was about,

But as I looked at my little friend's door, *the light had now gone out!*

Since he had left so suddenly, and without a warm goodbye…

I was left behind feeling really sad, and left me wondering *"Why?"*

Christmas would be different now, as he left us with the thought…

That happiness of loved ones, cannot be simply "bought".

The Christmas season that always comes with hopes for awesome toys,

Was now replaced with a different message for all the girls and boys…

But to my surprise, what I realized then, as I looked upon the tree,

A *"brand new"* ornament hanging there, *for everyone to see!*

It was hanging in a special place, where branches seemed to part...

It was the cutest *Christmas Gnome,* who now lives within *my heart!!*

FROM the AUTHOR:

As "Tim" brings you along on his latest adventure in the "Tim's Adventures" series, we hope you enjoy this heartwarming story and its worthwhile message that there is more to Christmas than the presents under the tree. It is our hope that you consider it a storybook worth sharing every Christmas with the entire family.

At this time of year, we would also like to extend our many thanks and appreciation for your continued support of "Tim" and his many adventures. We hope you continue to enjoy sharing his many encounters at your special family story time.

MERRY CHRISTMAS!